Events of

C000094049

News for every day

**The Boswell Sisters. Their hit song,
The Devil and the Deep Blue Sea, is
recorded on 21 March 1932.**

By Hugh Morrison

MONTPELIER PUBLISHING

Front cover (clockwise from left): Poster for the 1932 Olympics. Aldous Huxley's book *Brave New World*. Poster for the first England-India airline. The MG K sports car. The actress Joan Crawford.

Back cover (clockwise from top): Amy Johnson. US President Franklin Delano Roosevelt. Poster for India's first airline. Poster for the luxury Italian liner, SS *Rex*. Poster for the Mars Bar. The US Olympic speed skating team.

Image credits: APK, F Schmutzer, National Photo Collection of Israel, Catmanum, Thomas Wolf, Derek Harper, John Thaxter, David Stanley, Keith Just.

Published in Great Britain by Montpelier Publishing.
Printed and distributed by Amazon KDP.

ISBN: 9798525619524

January
1932

Friday 1: Ford motor cars go into production in the Soviet Union, under the NAZ marque.

Mahatma Gandhi informs India's Viceroy, Lord Willingdon, that he will restart his campaign of civil disobedience against British rule.

Saturday 2: Japanese forces in Manchuria capture Jinzhou.

Sunday 3: A diplomatic incident occurs as the US consul to Manchuria is assaulted and beaten by invading Japanese troops.

Monday 4: Indian independence activists Gandhi and Jawaharlal Nehru are arrested following resumption of anti-British activities.

The Department of Commerce Building opens on 4 January.

The largest office building in the world to this date, the Department of Commerce building in Washington, DC, opens.

The Archbishop of Canterbury forbids the remarriage of divorced persons in church.

January 1932

A regular air service between London and Cape Town, South Africa, begins on 20 January.

Tuesday 5: The author Umberto Eco (*The Name of the Rose*) is born in Alessandria, Italy (died 2016).

Wednesday 6: Joseph Lyons becomes Prime Minister of Australia.

Thursday 7: The US government first uses the Stimson Doctrine (non-recognition of states created by aggression) by refusing to recognise Japanese occupied Manchuria.

Friday 8: Japan's Emperor Hirohito survives an assassination attempt by a Korean nationalist in Tokyo.

Saturday 9: The German government announces it will not pay any more reparations to the Allies for the First World War, citing economic difficulties.

Sunday 10: Crown Prince Louis Rwagasore of Burundi is born (died 1961).

Monday 11: All meetings of more than five persons are banned by emergency decree in India, following Gandhi's call to resume civil disobedience.

Tuesday 12: Bulgaria joins Germany in declaring itself unable to meet war reparations payments.

Joseph Lyons becomes Prime Minister of Australia on 6 January.

Wednesday 13: Sophia of Prussia, Queen Consort of Greece and grand-daughter of Queen Victoria, dies aged 61.

Thursday 14: Ravel's *Piano Concerto in G Major* is first performed.

Friday 15: Linguistics professor Dr Allan Sinclair of Columbia University declares that US speech is degenerating into the 'jargon of the jungle' with slang phrases such as 'oh yeah' and 'OK' increasing in use.

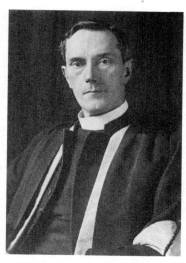

William Inge, Dean of St Paul's Cathedral, London, gives a controversial lecture on the afterlife on 17 January.

Saturday 16: Adolf Hitler is acquitted by a Berlin court on a charge of libel against Nazi party leadership challenger Walter Stennes.

Sunday 17: Bertolt Brecht's play *The Mother* opens in Berlin.

The Reverend William Ralph Inge, Dean of London's St Paul's cathedral, declares in a lecture that heaven is not a physical place but a 'kingdom of values.'

Monday 18: Authorities put out an urgent appeal for boats to evacuate 5000 people from flooding near Jackson, Mississippi.

Outbreaks of violence between republicans and monarchists take place across Spain.

Adolf Hitler is acquitted on 16 January following a libel case.

January 1932

The 'Bloomsbury Group' author Lytton Strachey dies on 21 January.

Tuesday 19: Ireland is hit by the worst flooding in thirty years.

Wednesday 20: Imperial Airways begins a regular air service between London and Cape Town; the trip takes ten days.

Thursday 21: Finland and the Soviet Union sign a non-aggression pact.

The writer and critic Lytton Strachey dies aged 51.

Friday 22: At least 10,000 people are killed in a peasant uprising in El Salvador.

Brooklyn's major league baseball team is officially named the Dodgers.

Saturday 23: Franklin D Roosevelt announces his candidacy for President of the United States.

Sunday 24: 100 convicts mutiny and take control of southwest England's Dartmoor prison for two hours.

Chinese military police defend Shanghai against invading Japanese forces.

he *Second Rhapsody* by ieorge Gershwin (above) is erformed on 29 January.

The Jesuit monastic order is banned in Spain and all members are ordered to leave the country.

Monday 25: Four miners are killed in an explosion at a mine in Llywnypia, Glamorganshire.

Tuesday 26: The Royal Navy submarine HMS *M2* sinks in the English Channel with the loss of all 60 hands.

William Wrigley Jr, creator of Wrigley's Spearmint Gum, dies aged 70.

Vednesday 27: HRH Prince Edward, Prince of Wales, is heckled y Indian independence protestors during a speech at the Albert lall in London.

'hursday 28: Japanese forces bomb the neutral Shanghai iternational Settlement; China appeals without success to the eague of Nations for assistance.

riday 29: George Gershwin's *Second Rhapsody* is performed or the first time, at the Symphony Hall in Boston.

iaturday 30: Chinese leader Chiang Kai-Shek mobilises Chinese forces against Japanese attack.

iunday 31: British and American warships are ordered to sail to ihanghai to evacuate expatriates.

February
1932

Monday 1: Aldous Huxley's dystopian novel *Brave New World* is published.

Tuesday 2: Duke Ellington and his Orchestra record the hit song *It Don't Mean A Thing If It Ain't Got That Swing.*

The film *Shanghai Express* starring Marlene Dietrich is released.

Wednesday 3: Austrian-born Adolf Hitler is officially declared a German citizen.

Thursday 4: The Winter Olympics opens in Lake Placid, New York.

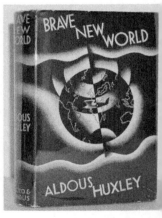

Brave New World **by Aldous Huxley is published on February**

Friday 5: Garfield Wood sets a world water speed record of 111.72 mph in *Miss America IX* on the Indian River, Florida.

Saturday 6: US troops arrive in Shanghai.

The French film director François Truffaut is born in Paris.

Sunday 7: 95 US citizens are evacuated from Nanking on board the USS *Simpson.*

Above: Marlene Dietrich stars in *Shanghai Express*, released on 2 February. Below: Edgar Wallace dies on 10 February.

Monday 8: American speed skater Irvin Jaffee wins the 10,000m at the Winter Olympics.

The composer John Williams is born in Floral Park, New York.

Tuesday 9: The Irish paramilitary Blueshirts group is formed, later merging with others to form the political party *Fine Gael*.

Wednesday 10: The crime writer Edgar Wallace (*The Four Just Men*) dies aged 56.

Thursday 11: Benito Mussolini meets with Pope Pius XI.

Friday 12: French husband and wife team Pierre and Andrée Brunet win their 2nd consecutive Olympic pairs figure skating gold medal at the Winter Olympics.

Saturday 13: Australian explorer Sir Douglas Mawson discovers Mount Hinks, Mount Marsden and the Rouse Islands in Antarctica.

Left: the US ladies' speed-skating team at the Winter Olympics.

February 1932

Commemorative stamp for the bicentenary of George Washington's birth, 22 February.

Sunday 14: Irish politician Patrick Reynolds is shot and fatally wounded following a doorstep argument with a former Royal Irish Constabulary policeman while canvassing for votes in Dublin.

Monday 15: The 84 year old German President, Paul von Hindenburg, announces he will stand again for election.

The Winter Olympics ends.

Tuesday 16: Fianna Fáil led by Éamon de Valera wins the Irish Free State general election.

Wednesday 17: After shooting a 'Mountie', Albert Johnson, the 'mad trapper of Rat River' is finally cornered by the Royal Canadian Mounted Police after a month-long nationwide manhunt. He is shot dead while resisting arrest.

Trotsky is banished from the USSR on 21 January after disagreements with leader Joseph Stalin.

Thursday 18: Frederick Augustus III, last king of Saxony, dies aged 66.

Friday 19: The British government establishes an emergency council in response to the Japanese invasion crisis in Shanghai.

Saturday 20: The controversial horror film *Freaks* is released.

Sunday 21: Leon Trotsky is officially banished from the Soviet Union.

Monday 22: Celebrations for the bicentennial of George Washington's birthday take place throughout the United States.

Malcolm Campbell in his record-breaking racing car, *Blue Bird*.

Tuesday 23: The US supreme court upholds a ban on cigarette advertising in the state of Utah.

Wednesday 24: Sir Malcolm Campbell sets the world land speed record at 253.96 mph in *Blue Bird* at Daytona Beach.

Thursday 25: Chinese authorities order all consuls to remove foreigners from Shanghai, as Japanese forces close in.

Elizabeth Taylor is born on 27 January.

Friday 26: The singer Johnny Cash is born in Kingsland, Arkansas (died 2003).

Saturday 27: The actress Elizabeth Taylor is born in London (died 2011).

Sunday 28: Heavy artillery battles begin between Japanese and Chinese forces on the outskirts of Shanghai.

Monday 29: Finnish troops clash with 5,000 members of the Lapua fascist party, attempting to march on Helsinki.

March
1932

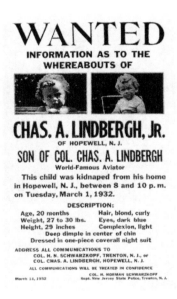

WANTED

INFORMATION AS TO THE
WHEREABOUTS OF

CHAS. A. LINDBERGH, JR.
OF HOPEWELL, N. J.

SON OF COL. CHAS. A. LINDBERGH
World-Famous Aviator

This child was kidnaped from his home
in Hopewell, N. J., between 8 and 10 p. m.
on Tuesday, March 1, 1932.

DESCRIPTION:

Age, 20 months	Hair, blond, curly
Weight, 27 to 30 lbs.	Eyes, dark blue
Height, 29 inches	Complexion, light

Deep dimple in center of chin
Dressed in one-piece coverall night suit

ADDRESS ALL COMMUNICATIONS TO
COL. H. N. SCHWARZKOPF, TRENTON, N. J., or
COL. CHAS. A. LINDBERGH, HOPEWELL, N. J.

ALL COMMUNICATIONS WILL BE TREATED IN CONFIDENCE

COL. H. NORMAN SCHWARZKOPF
March 11, 1932   Supt. New Jersey State Police, Trenton, N. J.

**Information poster from the
Lindbergh Baby kidnapping.**

Tuesday 1: Charles Lindbergh Jr, baby son of the aviator Charles Lindbergh, is kidnapped from his home in Amwell, New Jersey, and a note demanding a $50,000 ransom is left behind. A nationwide manhunt and media frenzy begins.

The cosmetic brand Revlon is founded.

Wednesday 2: Finnish troops move to put down the fascist uprising, as rebels seize the town of Mantsale near Helsinki.

Thursday 3: The Twentieth Amendment to the US Constitution is passed, moving the inauguration of Presidents from March to January.

Friday 4: The League of Nations votes unanimously to demand that Japanese forces withdraw from Shanghai.

**u Yi becomes Emperor of
Manchukuo on 9 March.**

**amon de Valera, Irish Free
tate leader.**

Saturday 5: Japanese nationalist extremists assassinate businessman Dan Takuma for alleged unpatriotic actitivities.

Sunday 6: The Finnish fascist rebellion is ended.

Charles Lindbergh receives a second ransom note for the return of his son, with the amount increased to $70,000.

The composer John Philip Sousa, who popularised the sousaphone, dies aged 77.

Monday 7: Four people are killed as unemployed protestors clash with police in Dearborn, Michigan.

The former Prime Minister of France, Aristide Briand, dies aged 69.

Tuesday 8: A retired schoolmaster, John Condon, is appointed to act as intermediary in the Lindbergh baby kidnapping case.

Wednesday 9: Pu Yi, the last Emperor of China, is installed by the Japanese as a puppet ruler in Manchukuo.

Éamon de Valera takes office as President of the Executive Council of the Irish Free State.

hursday 10: Kurt Weill's opera *Die Burgschaft* is first performed t the Berlin state opera house.

March 1932

The first trains, cars and cyclists cross the Sydney Harbour Bridge after its opening on 19 March.

Friday 11: Adolf Hitler quashes rumours that he is about to lead a coup in Germany, stating that the Nazi party has no intention to 'abandon the legal path' to power.

Saturday 12: John Condon, intermediary in the Lindbergh baby kidnapping, meets with an unidentified man in a New York cemetery to discuss handover of the ransom.

Sunday 13: In the German elections, Paul von Hindenburg is re-elected as Chancellor with 53% of the votes compared to Adolf Hitler's 36%.

Monday 14: George Eastman, photographic pioneer and creator of Kodak, commits suicide aged 77 after a long illness.

Tuesday 15: Shots are fired at Adolf Hitler and Joseph Goebbels on a train near Jena, Germany, but they escape unharmed.

The BBC makes its first radio transmissions from Broadcasting House in London.

Paul von Hindenburg is re-elected as Chancellor of Germany on 13 March.

Wednesday 16: John Condon, intermediary in the Lindbergh kidnapping case, is sent a baby's sleeping suit to prove that the kidnappers are genuine.

Thursday 17: The offices of the Nazi party across Germany are raided by police looking for evidence that Hitler is planning a coup.

Friday 18: Forbra wins the Grand National at 50-1.

Saturday 19: The Sydney Harbour Bridge is officially opened.

Cambridge wins the 84th Boat Race.

Sunday 20: Seven armed men are arrested in Havana, Cuba, after seizing control of the city's radio station and broadcasting communist propaganda.

Monday 21: A two-day tornado outbreak begins in the southern USA, killing 334 people.

Johnny Weissmuller stars as Tarzan in the film *Tarzan the Ape Man*, released on 25 March.

March 1932

Wheeler and Wolsey star in *Girl Crazy*, released on 27 March.

Tuesday 22: The Irish Free State government announces it has the right to remove the Oath of Allegiance to the British monarch.

Wednesday 23: Nazi and communist newspapers are temporarily banned from publication by the German government after claims they are putting the country's stability at risk.

Thursday 24: Station WABC in New York makes the world's first radio broadcast from a moving train.

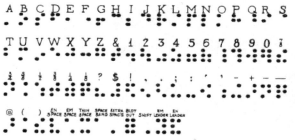

Left: Buford Green's Semagraph code, first demonstratd on 29 March. The Semagraph typewriter converts letters into a holepunch code which can be read by a photoelectric cell and converted into printing type.

Friday 25: *Tarzan the Ape Man*, the first of 12 Tarzan films starring Johnny Weissmuller in the title role, is released.

Saturday 26: The Japanese government announces it will leave the League of Nations if undue pressure is put on it to withdraw its troops from China.

Sunday 27: The musical film *Girl Crazy,* starring the comedy duo Wheeler and Woolsey, is released.

Jim Mollison breaks the London to Cape Town speed record on 28 March.

Monday 28: British pilot Jim Mollison, husband of Amy Johnson, flies from London to Cape Town in a record 4 days and 17 hours.

Tuesday 29: US inventor Buford L Green demonstrates the Semagraph, an automatic typesetting machine similar to a modern scanner. The technology does not go into general use until decades later.

Wednesday 30: The kidnappers of Charles Lindbergh's son increase their ransom demand to $100,000.

Thursday 31: Ford introduces the Flathead V8 engine, making 8-cylinder engines much more affordable for production motor cars.

April
1932

Friday 1: The investigation of the Lindbergh baby kidnapping becomes international, as detectives sail for England to pursue enquiries.

Saturday 2: The former Crown Prince of Germany, Wilhelm, endorses Adolf Hitler for President.

Sunday 3: After paying a $50,000 first ransom installment, negotiators in the Lindbergh baby abduction fail to find the child in the location given by the kidnappers.

Monday 4: The actor Anthony Perkins (*Psycho*) is born in New York City (died 1992).

Paul Muni stars in *Scarface*, released on 9 April.

Vitamin C is first isolated by CC King at the University of Pittsburgh.

mar Sharif is born on April.

Tuesday 5: German police claim to have found secret Nazi documents revealing plans to start a civil war.

Wednesday 6: The Danube Conference on the future of the remnants of the Austro-Hungarian Empire opens in London.

Thursday 7: During negotiations in the British Consulate, Japanese forces refuse to withdraw from Shanghai, claiming the League of Nations has no authority to order them to.

riday 8: *This is the Night*, the film in which Cary Grant makes s acting debut, is released.

aturday 9: The gangster film *carface* starring Paul Muni is leased.

he rock and roll musician Carl erkins is born in Tiptonville, ennessee (died 1998).

unday 10: The actor Omar harif is born in Alexandria, Egypt lied 2015).

onday 11: Thousands of people e forced to flee from their homes s fourteen volcanoes erupt in the ndes.

Greta Garbo and John Barrymore in *Grand Hotel*.

uesday 12: The drama film *Grand otel*, starring Greta Garbo and onel Barrymore premieres in New York City.

April 1932

Newcastle United forward Jack Allen scores twice in the FA Cup Final on 23 April.

Wednesday 13: The German government orders all paramilitary branches of the Nazi party to be dissolved with immediate effect.

Thursday 14: The worst rioting in New Zealand's history occurs when thousands of unemployed demonstrators clash with police in Auckland.

Friday 15: The governments of Bulgaria and Greece appeal to the League of Nations for aid after becoming unable to settle foreign debts.

Saturday 16: The US Congress debates whether to authorise the printing of $2bn to meet the military budget shortfall.

Sunday 17: Charles Duryea, the first car manufacturer in the USA, announces he has built a prototype car weighing only 500 pounds which can do 80 mpg; it is never put into production.

Monday 18: US Presidential candidate Franklin D Roosevelt announces that Prohibition should be a state rather than federal law.

Tuesday 19: Britain's Chancellor of the Exchequer Neville Chamberlain presents a budget which does not mention the $171.5m war debt owed to the USA.

Mussolini unveils a statue of Caesar in Rome on 21 April.

Wednesday 20: The first air-conditioned sleeper train goes into service, between St Louis, Missouri and New York City.

Thursday 21: Benito Mussolini dedicates a large statue of Julius Caesar in Rome on the anniversary of the city's founding.

Friday 22: The jailed gangster Al Capone offers to use his underworld contacts to return the kidnapped son of Charles Lindbergh, in exchange for release from prison.

Saturday 23: Newcastle United defeats Arsenal 2-1 in the FA Cup Final at Wembley Stadium.

The Shakespeare Memorial Theatre is opened in Stratford-upon-Avon.

The Kinder Scout mass trespass demonstration takes place on 24 April.

Sunday 24: The Nazi party makes large gains in local elections in Germany and Austria.

A mass trespass by ramblers takes place at Kinder Scout in England's Peak District, in protest against land access laws.

Monday 25: The actor William (Bill) Roache MBE is born in Nottingham. As Ken Barlow in *Coronation Street*, he becomes the longest serving male television actor in a continuous role.

Left: Bill Roache is born on 25 April.

April 1932

Tuesday 26: It is announced that if US government pensions for war veterans continue at the present rate, the equivalent of the entire US expenditure of the Great War will have been paid by 1945.

Wednesday 27: US President Herbert Hoover vetoes a bill to increase pensions for ex-servicemen.

The poet Hart Crane, pupil of TS Eliot, commits suicide aged 32.

Thursday 28: The Turkish president Mustafa Kemal Pasha arrives in the Soviet Union for a state visit.

Friday 29: A poll in the *Literary Digest* magazine shows only two US states, Kansas and North Carolina, are still in favour of Prohibition.

Saturday 30: Britain and the USA refuse to concede to a ban on all military ships over 10,000 tons at the Geneva arms reduction conference.

May
1932

Jack Benny's first radio show starts on 2 May.

Sunday 1: Protesters clash with police in London's Hyde Park after attempting to march on the Japanese embassy to demonstrate against the invasion of China.

Monday 2: Comedian Jack Benny hosts his first radio show, *The Canada Dry Program.*

Tuesday 3: The first Pulitzer Prize for drama is awarded, to George S Kaufman, Morrie Ryskind and Ira Gershwin for the musical *Of Thee I Sing.*

Wednesday 4: The gangster Al Capone begins an 11-year jail term for tax evasion.

Thursday 5: Japan and China sign the Shanghai Ceasefire Agreement.

Friday 6: President Paul Doumer is fatally wounded by a Russian assassin during a book fair in Paris.

May 1932

GEORGES PHILIPPAR
Nouveau Paquebot des Messageries Maritimes

The MS *Georges Philippar* sinks after catching fire on 16 May.

Saturday 7: Burgoo King wins the Kentucky Derby.

Sunday 8: 32 people are killed in landslides near Lyon, France.

Monday 9: The actress Geraldine McEwan (*Miss Marple*) is born in Old Windsor, Berkshire (died 2015).

Tuesday 10: British physicist James Chadwick discovers the neutron.

Wednesday 11: Britain warns the Irish Free State that it will lose preferential tariffs if it abolishes the Oath of Allegiance to the British sovereign.

Singer Alma Cogan is born on 19 May.

Thursday 12: The body of the kidnapped baby, Charles Lindbergh Jr, is found by chance just five miles from the Lindbergh home. The killer, Bruno Hauptmann, is later brought to justice and executed in 1935.

Friday 13: In Australia's first constitutional crisis, New South Wales leader Jack Lang becomes the first state premier to be dismissed by a state governor acting under the authority of the King.

Saturday 14: Burgoo King wins the Preakness Stakes.

Sunday 15: The Prime Minister of Japan, Inukai Tsuyoshi, is assassinated in Tokyo in an an attempted ultra-nationalist coup.

Monday 16: 54 people are killed when the French liner MS *Georges Phillipar* catches fire in the Gulf of Aden.

Tuesday 17: British troops finally quell four days of Hindu-Muslim rioting in Bombay, in which 88 people are killed.

Wednesday 18: Police in Cuba arrest hundreds of people involved in a plot to overthrow the government of Gerardo Machado.

Thursday 19: The singer Alma Cogan is born in London (died 1966).

Friday 20: 1070 people are killed in an earthquake in Torbet-I-heydarly, Persia.

Saturday 21: Amelia Earhart becomes the first woman to complete a solo crossing of the Atlantic by plane when she lands in Culmore, County Londonderry.

Amelia Earhart becomes the first woman to fly non-stop across the Atlantic on 21 May.

May 1932

Melvyn Douglas and Greta Garbo star in *As You Desire Me*, released on 28 May.

Sunday 22: Saito Makoto is appointed Prime Minister of Japan.

Monday 23: The US Congress rejects calls to legalise beer of up to 2.75% in volume.

Tuesday 24: The German parliament passes a motion that any attack on the free city-state of Danzig by Poland will be considered an attack on Germany.

Wednesday 25: Fighting breaks out in Germany's federal Prussian assembly between Nazis and communists.

Thursday 26: Alexandros Papanastasiou becomes Prime Minister of Greece.

Friday 27: The columnist and raconteur Jeffrey Bernard is born in London (died 1997).

Saturday 28: The film *As You Desire Me* starring Greta Garbo and Melvyn Douglas is released.

Sunday 29: The Nazi party wins the first absolute majority in a state election, winning 24 out of 48 seats in Oldenburg.

Monday 30: Heinrich Bruning resigns as German Chancellor, to be replaced by Franz von Papen.

Tuesday 31: Japan agrees to withdraw troops from Shanghai.

June
1932

Wednesday 1: April the Fifth wins the Epsom Derby.

Thursday 2: In Conroe, Texas, an attempt by a prosecution team to put a talking parrot – only witness of a double murder – on the stand is blocked by the judge.

Friday 3: Lou Gehrig becomes the first American League baseball player to hit four home runs in one game.

Lou Gehrig hits four home runs on 3 June.

Saturday 4: Italian police foil an assassination attempt on Benito Mussolini in Rome.

Sunday 5: Tazio Nuvolari wins the Italian Grand Prix.

Harmodio Arias Madrid becomes President of Panama.

Monday 6: Top income tax rates in the USA rise from 25% to 63%.

Tuesday 7: The airline Egyptair is founded.

June 1932

Ex-servicemen camp out in Washington, DC, demanding an increase in military pensions.

Wednesday 8: The Irish Free State parliament votes to retain the Oath of Allegiance to the King; it is removed in 1933.

Thursday 9: Adolf Hitler is fined 1000 marks for contempt of court in a libel case.

Friday 10: A failed assassination attempt is made on President Machado of Cuba.

Saturday 11: Mohammed Ali Bey al-Abad becomes the first President of Syria.

Sunday 12: The BBC begins its Scottish service from Westerglen transmitting station.

Monday 13: 15,000 US military veterans march on Washington in support of a proposed pension bonus.

Tuesday 14: The Danzig Crisis begins as Polish and British warships enter the neutral port of Danzig; the event is seen as an affront to the city's majority German population.

Wednesday 15: The Republican Party's national convention in Chicago votes in favour of maintaining the policy of Prohibition.

Thursday 16: The Lausanne Conference on German war reparations opens in Switzerland.

Friday 17: The US Senate votes against a pension bonus for veterans.

Boxing champ Jack Sharkey.

Saturday 18: The world's first 'peace park' opens on the US-Canadian border at Waterton Glacier.

Sunday 19: A counter-coup attempt takes place in Chile to try to restore the rule of President Marmaduke Grove, deposed on 16 June.

Monday 20: A tickertape parade takes place in New York City in honour of Amelia Earhart's completion of the first female solo flight across the Atlantic.

Tuesday 21: Jack Sharkey defeats Max Schmeling to win the World Heavyweight Boxing championship in Madison Square Garden.

Wednesday 22: US President Hoover proposes dramatic unilateral disarmament, including the banning of tanks and bomber planes.

The actress Prunella Scales (*Fawlty Towers, Great Canal Journeys*) is born in Sutton, Surrey.

Thursday 23: Pope Pius XI issues a ban on artificial flowers in church, and the taking of photographs during wedding ceremonies.

Friday 24: A bloodless coup in Siam ends with the absolute ruler, King Prajadhipok, agreeing to head a constitutional monarchy.

Prunella Scales is born on 22 June.

June 1932

The war drama *The Man from Yesterday* starring Claudette Colbert and Clive Brooke is released.

Saturday 25: The artist Sir Peter Blake, designer of the cover of the Beatles' *Sergeant Pepper's Lonely Hearts Club Band* album, is born in Dartford, Kent.

Sunday 26: One million people participate in the Eucharistic Congress of Dublin to celebrate the 1500th anniversary of St Patrick's arrival in Ireland.

Monday 27: A suspect in the Lindbergh baby kidnapping, hoaxer John F Curtis, is found guilty of obstructing justice by falsely claiming to have had contact with the kidnappers.

Tuesday 28: The Indian cricket team plays its first Test match at Lords, losing to England.

Wednesday 29: The US Democrat national convention votes to repeal Prohibition.

Thursday 30: In the Lausanne war reparations conference, France and Germany refuse to budge on the repayments deadlock.

India's cricket team plays its first Test at Lord's on 28 June.

July
1932

Friday 1: Franklin D Roosevelt is nominated as the Democratic US Presidential candidate.

Saturday 2: The actress Jean Harlow and actor Paul Bern are married in Beverley Hills, California.

Manuel II, last king of Portugal, dies aged 42.

The Anglepoise lamp is patented on 4 July.

Sunday 3: 12,000 members of the Iron Front, the liberal paramilitary organisation opposed to both communism and the Nazis, march in Berlin.

Monday 4: German pilot Hans Bertram and his mechanic Adolph Hausman are found alive after going missing in a remote part of northern Australia on 15 May.

British inventor George Carwardine patents the Anglepoise lamp.

July 1932

Salazar begins his 36-year rule of Portugal on 5 July.

Tuesday 5: Antonio de Oliveira Salazar becomes Prime Minister of Portugal. He goes on to rule for another 36 years.

Wednesday 6: The author Kenneth Grahame (*The Wind in the Willows*) dies aged 73.

Thursday 7: The French submarine *Prométhée* sinks off the north west coast of France with the loss of all hands.

Friday 8: The Reverend Harold Davidson, Rector of Stiffkey in Norfolk, is defrocked after allegations of improper conduct with young women. The case creates a tabloid sensation and Davidson becomes a street preacher in an attempt to clear his name; he dies in 1937 after being attacked by a lion in a publicity stunt.

The Dow Jones Industrial Average closes at 42.22 points, the lowest level of the Great Depression.

Saturday 9: The Lausanne Conference on German war reparations ends with an agreement that Germany will pay a full and final settlement of 3 billion gold marks.

Sunday 10: The militant anti-Nazi group, Antifascist Action, stages its first rally in Berlin.

Monday 11: Switzerland bans the wearing of Nazi uniforms.

Tuesday 12: Norway annexes Erik the Red's Land in eastern Greenland.

Kaye Don breaks the world water speed record on 18 July in *Miss England III*.

Wednesday 13: Amelia Earhart sets a world record for a solo female flight across the USA from Los Angeles to Newark in 19 hours and 40 minutes.

Thursday 14: Sir Edward Elgar conducts a recording of his cello concerto featuring 16-year old violinist Yehudi Menuhin.

Friday 15: The League of Nations agrees to loans to Austria on condition that it does not enter into any political agreements with Germany.

Saturday 16: Veterans known as the 'bonus army' riot in front of the White House in protest against the decision by Congress not to allow them to redeem their wartime pay bonuses until 1945.

Sunday 17: 18 people are killed in fighting between Nazis and communists in Hamburg, Germany.

Monday 18: All outdoor demonstrations are banned in Germany.

Kaye Don sets the world water speed record at 119.81 mph in *Miss England III* on Loch Lomond in Scotland.

Lambeth Bridge opens on 19 July.

Tuesday 19: King George V opens London's Lambeth Bridge.

Wednesday 20: German Chancellor Franz von Papen uses emergency powers to seize direct control of Prussia, Germany's largest state.

July 1932

Thursday 21: The British Empire Economic Conference opens in Ottawa, Canada.

Friday 22: The Broadway impresario Florenz Ziegfeld Jr, creator of the Ziegfeld Follies, dies aged 65.

Saturday 23: The six-month-long Geneva disarmament conference ends, with no major agreements on arms reduction.

Sunday 24: Nine people are killed during a police clampdown on communists in Havana, Cuba.

Monday 25: The USSR signs non-aggression pacts with Estonia, Finland and Poland.

Tuesday 26: 69 people are killed when the German training ship *Niobe* sinks in the Baltic.

Wednesday 27: Paul Gorguloff, assassin of the French President Paul Doumer, is sentenced to death.

Thursday 28: The US Hoover administration is attacked in the press for the heavy-handed dispersal of protesting military veterans in Washington.

Top: poster for *White Zombie*, released on 28 July.
Above: Florenz Ziegfeld Jr dies on 22 July.

The first full-length zombie film, *White Zombie* starring Bela Lugosi, is released.

Friday 29: In Hungary, two communist leaders are tried and hanged for treason on the same day, prompting international outrage.

Saturday 30: The 1932 Summer Olympics open in Los Angeles, California.

Sunday 31: The Nazi party wins the German federal elections.

Andre Leducq wins the Tour de France.

Above left: poster for the 1932 Summer Olympics, which opens on 30 July
Above right: Andre Leducq wins the Tour de France on 31 July.

August
1932

Monday 1: The first quarter bearing the head of George Washington is issued in the US.

The first Mars Bar is produced in Slough, England.

Tuesday 2: Britain's Tommy Hampson wins Gold for the 800 metres in the Los Angeles Olympics.

The actor Peter O'Toole is born (died 2013).

The Washington quarter is first issued on 1 August.

Wednesday 3: 19 Latin American countries express official disapproval of fighting between Bolivian and Paraguayan troops in the Gran Chaco region.

Thursday 4: Benito Mussolini announces in a newspaper editorial that pacifism is cowardice.

Left: Peter O'Toole is born on 2 August.

oster for Rin Tin Tin's last film,
eleased in 1931. The canine star
es on 10 August.

Friday 5: The Barrow Gang, famous for its members Bonnie and Clyde, claim their first victim as Deputy Sheriff Eugene Moore is shot dead in Stringtown, Oklahoma.

Saturday 6: Germany's first Autobahn opens, linking the cities of Bonn and Cologne.

Sunday 7: Soviet leader Joseph Stalin declares all property on collective farms to belong to the state, with the death penalty for unauthorised use.

Monday 8: The US radio pioneer Harry Shoemaker dies aged 53.

Tuesday 9: Germany ntroduced draconian new laws to prevent riots following a wave f civil disorder across the country.

Wednesday 10: The German Shepherd anine film star, Rin Tin Tin, dies aged 2.

Thursday 11: US President Herbert Hoover begins his re-election campaign y stating in a speech that Prohibition hould be left up to individual states.

Friday 12: Queen Sirikit of Thailand is orn in Bangkok.

Queen Sirikit the Queen Mother of Thailand is born on 12 August.

August 1932

August Piccard with his balloon capsule.

Saturday 13: 40 people die when a hurricane hits Freeport, Texas.

Sunday 14: The Los Angeles Olympics closes, with the USA in top place with 41 gold medals.

Monday 15: London Underground's rebuilt Marble Arch station is opened.

Tuesday 16: The British Raj widens Indian suffrage under the Communal Award, giving the vote to previously disenfranchised groups including the 'untouchable' caste.

Wednesday 17: Hindu nationalists in India attack the new Communal Award, claiming it is a 'divide and rule' policy of the British.

Thursday 18: Auguste Piccard and Max Cosyns set a new altitude record by ascending over 10 miles in a hot air balloon in Switzerland.

Friday 19: British pilot Jim Mollison completes the first solo east-west crossing of the Atlantic, flying from Ireland to Canada in 30 hours 10 minutes.

Frederic March is voted 'favourite actor' on 21 August.

Saturday 20: The British Empire Economic Conference in Ottawa, Canada, ends.

Sunday 21: The first Venice International Film Festival closes, with Frederic March voted 'favourite actor' for *Dr Jekyll and Mr Hyde.*

Monday 22: BBC television makes its first experimental broadcast.

Tuesday 23: A transatlantic air race begins between the USA, Canada and Norway.

Wednesday 24: Thor Solberg and Carl Peterson, the Norwegian transatlantic air race team, crash in Newfoundland but escape unhurt.

Hermann Göring becomes Reichstag President on 30 August.

Thursday 25: General Jose Sanjurjo is sentenced to life imprisonment for attempting to overthrow the Spanish republic.

Friday 26: Fritz Sauckel becomes the first Nazi to serve as head of a German landtag (regional state).

Saturday 27: 200,000 cotton workers go out on strike in Lancashire in the north of England.

Sunday 28: The San Marino Fascist Party wins a unanimous victory in the European microstate's general election.

Monday 29: The Soviet Union introduces the death penalty for theft, in an attempt to curb a rising crime wave.

Tuesday 30: Hermann Göring is elected President of the Reichstag (German parliament).

Wednesday 31: The German government sends a memorandum to France stating that unless France disarms, Germany will re-arm in contravention of the Treaty of Versailles.

The entertainer and musician Roy Castle is born in Kirklees, West Yorkshire (died 1994).

September 1932

Thursday 1: Peru and Colombia threaten to go to war when armed Peruvians seize the city of Leticia.

Friday 2: At least 23,000 people are made homeless in Texas and Mexico when the Rio Grande floods following severe rainfall.

Saturday 3: A new air speed record of 296.287 mph is set by Major James Doolittle in the US national air race held at Cleveland, Ohio.

Patsy Cline is born on 8 September.

Sunday 4: A three-day international peace conference opens in Vienna.

Monday 5: The Stresa Conference on the future of central and eastern Europe opens in Italy.

Tuesday 6: An attempted fascist coup by the Ustase paramilitary organisation is put down in Yugoslavia.

Wednesday 7: The philanthropist John Paul Getty Jr is born in Genoa, Italy (died 2003).

Joan Crawford.

Thursday 8: The Spanish government announces all aristocratic property is to be confiscated.

The singer Patsy Cline (*Your Cheating Heart*) is born in Winchester, Virginia (died 1963).

Friday 9: War breaks out between Bolivia and Paraguay.

The drama film *Rain* starring Joan Crawford premieres in Hollywood.

Saturday 10: The defrocked Anglican priest Harold Davidson is fined in Blackpool, England, for staging a publicity stunt seated in a barrel on the seafront.

Sunday 11: Manmohan Singh, the first Sikh Prime Minister of India, is born in Gah, Punjab.

Monday 12: The German parliament passes a vote of no confidence in Chancellor Franz von Papen's government.

Tuesday 13: The New York Yankees defeat the Cleveland Indians 9-3 to win baseball's American League.

Wednesday 14: 55 people are killed when a French military train crashes in Algeria.

Paul Gorguloff, assassin of the French Prime Minister Paul Doumer, is executed.

Thursday 15: Germany introduces a 40-hour work week in an attempt to create more jobs.

Friday 16: The British test pilot Cyril Uwins sets a world altitude record of 8.5 miles (13,404m) in a Vickers Vespa biplane.

September 1932

The actress Peg Entwistle commits suicide on 18 September by jumping from the letter 'H' of the Hollywood sign in Los Angeles.

Saturday 17: The Han Liu War begins in China between rival warlords Han Fuju and Liu Zhennian.

Sunday 18: The body of the actress Peg Entwistle is found after she commits suicide by jumping from the 'H' of the 'Hollywood' sign above Los Angeles.

Monday 19: Bolivia and Paraguay agree to peace talks following the outbreak of war between them on 9 September.

Tuesday 20: Garfield Wood sets the world water speed record of 124.86mph on the St Clair River in Miss America X.

Mahatma Gandhi begins a hunger strike against the new British rules on Indian suffrage.

The Methodist Church is unified in Britain with a merger of the separate Primitive, Wesleyan and United denominations.

The pianist Glenn Gould is born on 25 September.

Wednesday 21: The writer Shirley Conran (*Superwoman, Lace*) is born in London.

Thursday 22: The government of the Japanese puppet state of Manchuria, China, demands international recognition within six months.

Friday 23: The Kingdom of Hejaz and Nejd is renamed Saudi Arabia.

Saturday 24: Per Albin Hansson becomes Prime Minister of Sweden.

Sunday 25: The pianist Glenn Gould is born in Toronto, Canada (died 1982).

Monday 26: Gandhi ends his hunger strike as the British government agrees to increase the rights of the Untouchable caste.

Tuesday 27: The award-winning Italian ocean liner SS Rex is launched.

Wednesday 28: Four members of the British government resign in protest at Prime Minister Ramsay Macdonald's tariff policy.

Thursday 29: Pope Pius XI issues the encyclical *Acerba Anime*, condemning the persecution of Catholics in Mexico.

Friday 30: The actor Ray Milland marries Frances Weber in Riverside, California.

Poster for the award-winning Italian liner, SS *Rex*, launched on 27 September.

October
1932

Saturday 1: Oswald Mosley founds the British Union of Fascists (BUF).

Sunday 2: The New York Yankees win baseball's World Series with a 13-6 victory over the Chicago Cubs.

Monday 3: Iraq is granted independence from Great Britain.

The Times newspaper is relaunched with the specially created Times New Roman typeface.

Oswald Mosley founds th
BUF on 1 Octobe

Tuesday 4: A three-month-long military rebellion against the Brazilian government is put down.

Wednesday 5: Crown Prince Michael of Romania makes a state visit to France.

Thursday 6: The Mexican state of Veracruz strips Catholic priests of citizenship and seizes all church property.

Friday 7: The London Philharmonic Orchestra gives its first performance.

The Italian liner SS *Rex* crosses the Atlantic in the record time of five days and fourteen hours.

The comedy duo Bob Hope and Bing Crosby, shown here with actress Marquita Rivera, meet for the first time on 14 October.

Saturday 8: The Royal Indian Air Force is formed.

The snooker player Ray Reardon is born in Tregarder, Monmouthshire.

Sunday 9: The Blue Star liner *Africstar* collides with the Norwegian vessel *Charente* off the coast of Dungeness in the English Channel.

Monday 10: Lee Bong-Chang is hanged for the attempted assassination of Crown Prince Hirohito of Japan.

Tuesday 11: The centenary of the invention of the telegraph is celebrated by the sending of the message 'What God hath wrought' around the world in a record 4 minutes 45 seconds.

Wednesday 12: One person is killed and 31 injured after a demonstration by 10,000 unemployed men turns violent in Belfast, Northern Ireland.

Thursday 13: Former British Prime Minister David Lloyd George declares there is 'imminent danger of a new world war' as reparations talks with Germany stall.

Left: David Lloyd George warns of impending war on 13 October.

October 1932

Albert Einstein makes a controversial announcement on 16 October.

Friday 14: The entertainment duo Bob Hope and Bing Crosby meet for the first time, at the New York Friars Club.

Saturday 15: Air India goes into operation, under the name Tata Airlines.

Sunday 16: During a lecture in Berlin, Albert Einstein upsets scientific consensus when he proposes that the earth is 10 billion years old instead of the 3 billion years previously thought.

Monday 17: Mexico bans immigration of 'prohibited' ethnic groups, including blacks, asians, gypsies and Hindus.

Tuesday 18: Britain abolishes its trade treaty with the Soviet Union.

Wednesday 19: Henry Ford endorses Herbert Hoover for re-election in the US Presidential race.

Thursday 20: The second serious riot within a week breaks out in Kingston Penitentiary, Ontario, Canada.

Friday 21: A third riot takes place in Kingston Penitentiary, this time requiring troops to be sent in to restore order.

Saturday 22: Charles de Brocqueville becomes Prime Minister of Belgium.

George Lansbury takes over Britain's Labour party on 25 October.

Left: Indian businessman JRD Tata starts India's first airline on 15 October.

Sunday 23: Italian leader Benito Mussolini proposes a Four Power Pact between Britain, France, Germany and Italy.

Monday 24: Thousands of Hunger March unemployed demonstrators clash with Oswald Mosley's fascists in central London.

Tuesday 25: George Lansbury is elected leader of Britain's Labour Party.

Wednesday 26: Charlie Chaplin wins a court action against his ex-wife Lita Grey, preventing her from allowing their children to appear in a film.

Thursday 27: Benito Mussolini opens the Exhibition of the Fascist Revolution in Rome's Palace of Expositions.

Friday 28: Tiburcio Carias Andino is elected President of Honduras.

Saturday 29: The 'Turco-Egyptian Hat Incident' takes place; a diplomatic row is caused when the Egyptian ambassador is told to remove his fez – a hat banned in Turkey – during a state function. He leaves in protest and later receives an apology.

Sunday 30: Arturo Allessandri becomes President of Chile.

Monday 31: Boxer Jackie Brown defeats Victor Perez to gain the World Flyweight title in Lancashire.

November
1932

Tuesday 1: James McNeill, first Governor-General of the Irish Free State, resigns in protest over disputes with Republican politicians.

200,000 Lancashire cotton workers go out on strike for higher pay.

Wednesday 2: 12 people are killed in fighting between communists and Nazis in Hamburg, Germany.

Thursday 3: Panagis Tsaldaris becomes Prime Minister of Greece.

Friday 4: Three people are killed in rioting in Berlin, Germany, following a transport strike.

Northern Ireland's Parliament building is opened on 16 November.

Saturday 5: The Lancashire cotton strike ends as workers agree to a pay cut.

Sunday 6: In Germany's Federal election, the Nazis lose 35 seats but retain overall control of Parliament.

Monday 7: The US Supreme Court decides Powell *v* Alabama, overturning the convictions of a group of black youths known as the Scottsboro Boys who were arrested for an attack on two white women in 1931.

Tuesday 8: Franklin D Roosevelt defeats incumbent Herbert Hoover in the US Presidential election.

Poster for the Academy Award-nominated film *I am a Fugitive from a Chain Gang*, released on 10 November.

Wednesday 9: 13 people are killed in clashes between communists and fascists in Geneva, Switzerland.

Thursday 10: The crime drama *I am a Fugitive from a Chain Gang* starring Paul Muni is released.

Friday 11: A large state funeral takes place in Moscow for Nadezhda Alliluyeva, wife of leader Joseph Stalin.

Saturday 12: 25 miners are killed in an explosion at Edge Green Colliery, Ashton-in-Makerfield, Lancashire.

Sunday 13: The Colorado River is diverted, the first major step in the construction of the Hoover Dam.

Monday 14: San Francisco police are ordered to stop all liquor raids in anticipation of the repeal of Prohibition .

November 1932

Franklin Delano Roosevelt is victorious in the US Presidential election on 8 November.

Tuesday 15: The singer and actress Petula Clark is born in Epsom, Surrey.

Wednesday 16: Northern Ireland's Stormont parliament building is opened by HRH the Prince of Wales.

Thursday 17: Franz von Papen resigns as Chancellor of Germany.

Friday 18: *Grand Hotel* wins Best Picture at the 5th Academy Awards.

The aviatrix Amy Johnson completes a flight from South Africa to England in a record-breaking 4 days 6 hours and 55 minutes.

Saturday 19: The third Round Table Conference on Indian independence opens in London.

Sunday 20: A bomb plot to assassinate French president Edouard Herriot is thwarted with an hour to spare.

Monday 21: German President von Hindenburg offers the Chancellorship to Adolf Hitler, who turns it down because he does not want to lead a coalition government.

Petula Clark is born on November

Tuesday 22: The actor Robert Vaughan (*The Man from UNCLE*) is born in New York City (died 2016).

Above: Amy Johnson, who makes a record-breaking solo flight from South Africa to England on 18 November.

Wednesday 23: The banished ex-communist party member Leon Trotsky arrives in Denmark for a lecture tour, where he is met by 300 communists protesting against his arrival.

Thursday 24: Special Thanksgiving church services take place across the USA to mark the bicentenary of George Washington's birth.

Friday 25: Mexico's persecution of Catholics continues, as an arrest order is made for all priests in the city of Monterey.

Saturday 26: The song *Brother, Can You Spare a Dime?* by Bing Crosby hits number one in the US record charts.

Sunday 27: Domnall Ua Buachalla becomes Governor General of the Irish Free State.

Monday 28: HM King George V holds a special audience with the Chancellor of the Exchequer, Neville Chamberlain, to discuss the impending war debt repayment deadline of approximately £30bn to the USA.

Right: Fred Astaire stars in *The Gay Divorce*, his last Broadway show, which opens on 29 November.

November 1932

Tuesday 29: The Cole Porter musical *Gay Divorce*, featuring the hit song *Night and Day*, opens on Broadway.

Wednesday 30: The Cecil B DeMille historical epic *The Sign of the Cross* premieres at New York City's Rialto Theatre.

The Soviet Union permits emigration of its citizens, but only in exchange for large financial sums.

December 1932

Thursday 1: The British government delivers a note to the United States asking for cancellation of all war debts, due to financial difficulties cause by the Great Depression.

Friday 2: The drama film *A Farewell to Arms* starring Gary Cooper and Helen Hayes is released.

The 1932/3 Ashes cricket season opens in Australia. It is the first in which the English team uses the controversial tactic of bodyline bowling (bowling directly at the batsman).

Saturday 3: Kurt von Schleicher becomes Chancellor of Germany.

Left: Gary Cooper and Helen Hayes in *A Farewell to Arms*, released on 2 December.

December 1932

Sunday 4: Italy announces a plan to electrify 40% of its railway network.

Monday 5: The 21st Amendment to the United States Constitution (the scrapping of Prohibition) is formally proposed in Congress. The ban on alcohol ends in December 1933.

The comic strip character Jane first appears in Britain's *Daily Mirror* newspaper.

Tuesday 6: Albert Einstein is granted a visa to visit the United States, following the quashing of rumours that he has communist connections.

Wednesday 7: Six people are injured and extensive damage caused after brawling breaks out in the German parliament between Nazis and communists.

The risqué cartoon character 'Jane' first appears on 5 December.

Thursday 8: The British horticulturalist and garden designer Gertrude Jekyll dies aged 89.

Friday 9: Japanese forces invade the Chinese province of Jehol.

Saturday 10: Britain's John Galsworthy is awarded the Nobel Prize for literature; Germany's Werner Heisenberg wins the award for physics.

Siam (now Thailand) becomes a constitutional monarchy under King Prajadhipok.

Right: John Galsworthy, author of *The Forsyte Saga*, is awarded the Nobel Prize for Literature on 10 December.

P Boncour becomes Prime
inister of France on 18
ecember.

Sunday 11: A peace treaty is negotiated between the USA, Britain, France, Germany and Italy resolving that no disputes between them be settled by force.

Monday 12: Diana Spencer-Churchill, daughter of Sir Winston Churchill, marries Sir John Milner Bailey.

China and Russia resume diplomatic relations following peace talks in Geneva.

Tuesday 13: A large increase in the US op and barley harvest for brewing is reported, as many farmers ave grown the crops in anticipation of the repeal of Prohibition.

Wednesday 14: The French government collapses in dispute ver US war debt repayments.

Thursday 15: France, Poland, Belgium, Estonia and Hungary efault on their US war debts.

Friday 16: 14 people are killed during a major fire in the Shirokiya epartment Store, Tokyo, Japan. The incident gives rise to an nduring myth that women died rather than jump to safety, for ar of their kimonos riding up.

wo former Argentinian presidents are arrested as a plot to verthrow the government is uncovered.

emale suffrage is introduced in Uruguay.

Saturday 17: A Hindu monk, Adhva Dut Swami, begins a hunger rike in Bombay, India, in opposition to Mahatma Gandhi's ampaign to give civil rights to the Untouchable caste.

Sunday 18: The first major indoor football game takes place in e USA when a Chicago Bears *v.* Portsmouth Spartans match

December 1932

Poster for *The Mummy*, starring Boris Karloff, released on 22 December.

has to be held in the Chicago Stadium due to severe bad weather.

Joseph-Paul Boncour becomes Prime Minister of France.

Monday 19: The BBC Empire Service (later renamed the World Service) begins broadcasting radio to the British Empire.

Tuesday 20: A 7.2 magnitude earthquake hits the Cedar Mountains region of Nevada.

Wednesday 21: The US Congress allows the production of beer of up to 3.2% volume.

HM King George V makes his first Christmas speech on 25 December.

Thursday 22: The horror film *The Mummy* starring Boris Karloff is released.

Friday 23: The first telephone link between Hawaii and the continental USA is opened.

Saturday 24: 54 people are killed in a mine explosion in Moweaqua, Illinois.

Sunday 25: HM King George V makes the first King's Christmas Speech to Britain and her Empire via radio. The speech is written by Rudyard Kipling.

Lt Gen Chesty Puller (shown here in 1950) puts down an uprising in Nicaragua on 26 December.

Monday 26: Forces led by the US army's most decorated officer, Lewis 'Chesty' Puller, are victorious in the Battle of El Sauce, an uprising against the US occupation of Nicaragua.

Tuesday 27: New York City's Radio City Music Hall opens.

Wednesday 28: The Soviet Union introduces compulsory passports for internal travel for everyone aged over 16.

The politician Roy Hattersley is born in Sheffield, England.

The stunning foyer of Radio City Music Hall, which opens on 27 December.

December 1932

Thursday 29: The US Congress approves the granting of independence for the Philippines by 1944, a date later delayed by two years due to the outbreak of the Second War.

Friday 30: 800 communists are arrested in Romania for subversive activities.

Saturday 31: The Soviet Union's first Five Year Plan comes to an end.

John Boles and Irene Dunn star in the comedy-drama film *Back Street,* released on 28 December.

Other titles from Montpelier Publishing:

A Little Book of Limericks:
Funny Rhymes for all the Family
ISBN 9781511524124

Scottish Jokes: A Wee Book of
Clean Caledonian Chuckles
ISBN 9781495297366

The Old Fashioned Joke Book:
Gags and Funny Stories
ISBN 9781514261989

Non-Religious Funeral Readings:
Philosophy and Poetry for Secular
Services
ISBN 9781500512835

Large Print Jokes: Hundreds of
Gags in Easy-to-Read Type
ISBN 9781517775780

**Spiritual Readings for Funerals
and Memorial Services**
ISBN 9781503379329

Victorian Murder: True Crimes,
Confessions and Executions
ISBN 9781530296194

Large Print Prayers: A Prayer for
Each Day of the Month
ISBN 9781523251476

**A Little Book of Ripping Riddles
and Confounding Conundrums**
ISBN 9781505548136

Vinegar uses: over 150 ways to use
vinegar
ISBN 9781512136623

Large Print Wordsearch:
100 Puzzles in Easy-to-Read Type
ISBN 9781517638894

The Pipe Smoker's Companion
ISBN 9781500441401

The Book of Church Jokes
ISBN 9781507620632

Bar Mitzvah Notebook
ISBN 9781976007781

Jewish Jokes
ISBN 9781514845769

Large Print Address Book
ISBN 9781539820031

How to Cook Without a Kitchen:
Easy, Healthy and Low-Cost Meals
ISBN 9781515340188

Large Print Birthday Book
ISBN 9781544670720

Retirement Jokes
ISBN 9781519206350

Take my Wife: Hilarious Jokes of
Love and Marriage
ISBN 9781511790956

Welsh Jokes: A Little Book of
Wonderful Welsh Wit
ISBN 9781511612241

1001 Ways to Save Money: Thrifty
Tips for the Fabulously Frugal!
ISBN 9781505432534

Available online at Amazon

Printed in Great Britain
by Amazon